Content

What is the *Tour de France*? 2

How long is the *Tour de France*? 4

What do the cyclists have to do? 6

What is a special jersey? 10

What do the cyclists wear? 12

What are the bikes like? 14

Do the cyclists have help? 16

Who is the winner? 18

Who can ride in the *Tour de France*? 20

Tour de France checklist 23

Index 24

What is the *Tour de France*?

The *Tour de France* is a big bike race. It is held in France each year. It is the most famous bike race in the world. It is 21 days long.

The Tour de France *is the most famous bike race in the world.*

Cyclists come from all over the world to race in the *Tour de France*. It is famous because it is very long and very hard. It goes all around France. Its name in English is "the tour of France".

The Tour de France *goes all around France.*

How long is the *Tour de France*?

The *Tour de France* is almost 4000 kilometres (km) long. It is made up of 21 stages. Each stage is about 180 km long.

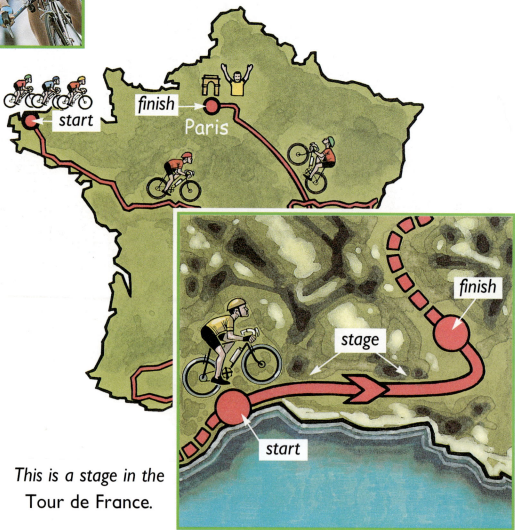

This is a stage in the Tour de France.

The cyclists in the *Tour de France* race in teams. Each team has nine cyclists in it. The cyclists all try to win points.

The cyclists race in teams.

What do the cyclists have to do?

The cyclists have to race up high mountains. The mountains are very high and very hard to ride up. There could be snow on top. The first cyclist to get to the top of a mountain wins points.

The cyclists have to ride up mountains.

Then the cyclists have to race down the other side of the mountains. This is very dangerous. The cyclists have to ride down very fast. They go at about 100 km per hour.

The cyclists have to ride down mountains.

The cyclists race along flat roads, too. This is hard because the cyclists must keep going fast for a long time.

The cyclists race along flat roads.

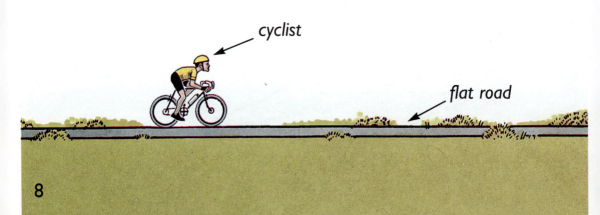

Some stages end with a sprint finish. Cyclists sprint by riding very, very fast. The sprint finish is the last kilometre of a stage. It is very dangerous because cyclists might crash into each other.

This is a sprint finish.

What is a special jersey?

At the end of each day, the three best cyclists of the day are given a special jersey to wear. They wear the special jersey on the next day of the race. The yellow jersey is worn by the cyclist who was the fastest.

The yellow jersey is worn by the cyclist who was fastest.

The green jersey is worn by the cyclist who won the most points. There are 35 points for the winner of a flat stage. There are 25 points for the winner of a mountain stage. There are extra points for the first cyclist to get to the top of a mountain.
The red and white jersey is worn by the cyclist who is the best at riding up mountains.

The green jersey is worn by the cyclist who won the most points.

The red and white jersey is worn by the cyclist who is the best at riding up mountains.

What do the cyclists wear?

At the bottom of a mountain it can be very hot, but at the top of the mountain it can be very cold. The cyclists have to wear special clothes. They wear special clothes so that they are cool when it is hot and warm when it is cold.

Cyclists wear special clothes so that they are cool when it is hot.

Cyclists wear special clothes so that they are warm when it is cold.

Here are some of the clothes that a cyclist could wear.

What are the bikes like?

The cyclists have to ride special bikes. The bikes have to race in the wind, rain and snow. The bikes have to race up and down high mountains and to race on flat roads.

Cyclists have to ride special bikes.

Here is a special bike that a cyclist could use.

Do the cyclists have help?

The cyclists need help to keep riding all day, so each team has helpers. The helpers ride in cars behind the cyclists. They can ride next to the cyclists, too. The helpers have other bikes and new bike parts for the cyclists. They have special food and drink for the cyclists, too.

Helpers ride next to a cyclist.

The cyclists need to have special food and drink. They need water, too.

A cyclist has a drink.

Who is the winner?

The winner of the *Tour de France* is the cyclist who wins the most points. The winner has to race fast and ride up mountains very well. The winner has to ride for a long time and ride fast, too. The winner also has to "grab the wheel" if he can.

Cyclists "grab the wheel".

"Grabbing the wheel" is riding just behind a cyclist to keep out of the wind. The cyclists want to "grab the wheel" because riding into the wind makes them tired.

Who can ride in the *Tour de France*?

Most of the cyclists are from 20 to 35 years old. They are the best cyclists in the world.

The Tour de France *cyclists are the best in the world.*

Not all cyclists can finish this race. Some cyclists crash and can't finish it. Some cyclists get hurt and can't finish it. Some cyclists get too tired and can't finish it.

This is a big crash.

Many cyclists think that the *Tour de France* is the hardest bike race in the world. Just to finish the *Tour de France* is almost as good as to win it!

The *Tour de France* is a hard race to win.

Tour de France checklist

Time .. 21 days

Km .. about 4000 km

Stages .. 21

Team .. 9 cyclists

First Tour de France .. 1903

Index

B
bikes 14

C
clothes 12, 13

D
drink 16, 17

F
food 16, 17

G
"grabbing the wheel"
..........................18, 19

H
helpers 16

J
jersey, green 11
jersey, red and white ..11
jersey, yellow 10

P
points 5, 6, 11, 18

S
sprint finish 9

T
team 5, 16